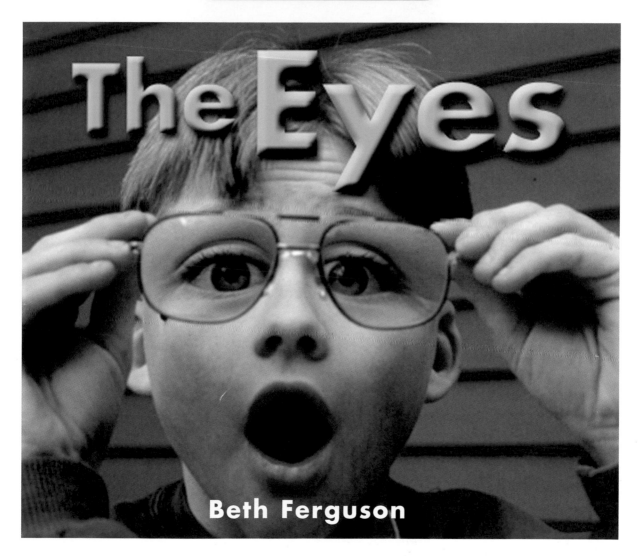

The Eyes

Beth Ferguson

BENCHMARK BOOKS

MARSHALL CAVENDISH
NEW YORK

Benchmark Books
Marshall Cavendish
99 White Plains Rd.
Tarrytown, NY 10591
www.marshallcavendish.com

Library of Congress Cataloging-in-Publication Data

Ferguson, Beth, 1968–
  The Eyes / Beth Ferguson.
      v. cm. — (Kaleidoscope)
Includes bibliographical references and index.
Contents: Eyes are for seeing — All about eyes — Inside your eyes —
How your eyes work — When eyes need help — Keeping eyes healthy.
  ISBN 0-7614-1590-4
  1. Eye—Juvenile literature. [1. Eye. 2. Vision. 3. Senses and
sensation.] I. Title. II. Series: Kaleidoscope (Tarrytown, N.Y.)
QP475.7.F47 2003   612.8'4—dc21   2003000650

Photo research by Anne Burns Images

Cover photo: Photo Researchers Inc./BSIP/Science Source

The photographs in this book are used with permission and through the courtesy of:
Superstock: title page. *Corbis:* Rolf Bruderer, 4; Mark L. Stephenson, 8; 23; Richard Townshend, 31; John-Marshall
Mantel, 32; Tom & Dee Ann McCarthy, 43. *Custom Medical Stock Photo:* 7, 11, 39. *Photo Researchers Inc./Science
Photo Library:* John Bavosi, 12, 16; Professor P. Motta, Department of Anatomy, Universitá La Sapienza, Rome, 19;
M. Dohrn, 20. *Phototake:* 15, 24, 27, 28. *Cajun Images:* Charles Martin, 35, 40. Photo Edit Inc.: Mary Kate Denny, 36.

Series design by Adam Mietlowski

Printed in Italy

6 5 4 3 2 1

Contents

Eyes Are for Seeing

It's hard to imagine what life would be like without eyes. Every day, you use your eyes to identify the faces of friends, to look both ways before crossing the street, and to read what your teacher writes on the chalkboard.

Without your eyes, you could not catch a baseball or see the colors of a rainbow. You would even have trouble knowing whether it is day or night. Even though you have four other senses—hearing, touch, taste, and smell—80 percent of all the information you receive about the world around you comes from what you see.

◀ *Think of all the ways you use your eyes every day.*

All About Eyes

When you look at your face in a mirror, you can only see a little bit of each eyeball. The human eye is about the size of a Ping-Pong ball, but most of it is hidden below your skin. Six muscles are attached to each eyeball. They allow you to move your eyes left and right or up and down without moving your head. This makes it easier to read across the pages of a book.

Each eyeball sits in a circular socket in your skull. The thick, heavy bone of the skull helps protect your soft, delicate eyes. Several other body parts also help keep your eyes safe. Your eyebrows soak up sweat and rain, so they will not flow into your eyes. Your eyelashes flick away tiny bits of dirt and dust.

The muscles attached to your eyeballs allow you to move your eyes in any direction you want.

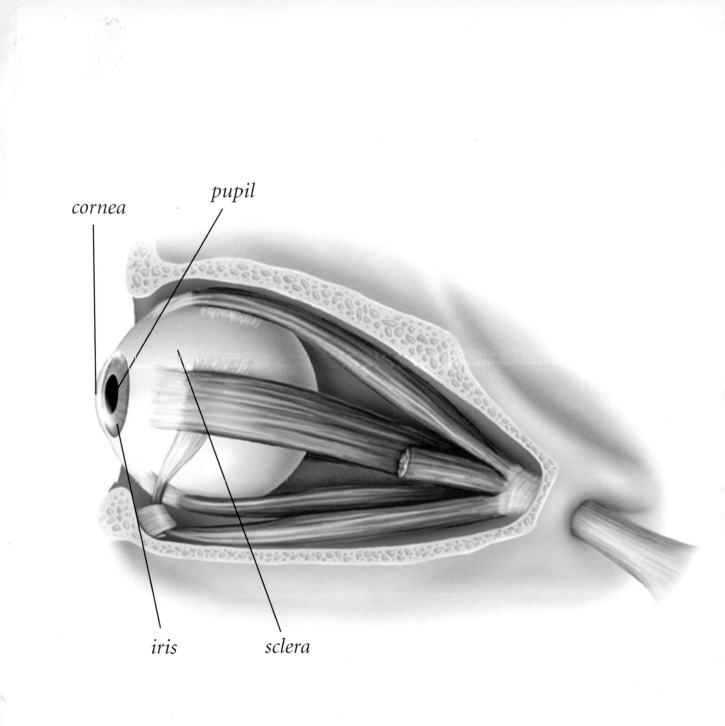

cornea

pupil

iris

sclera

Your eyelids blink more than nine hundred times every hour. Each time they close, your eyelids sweep across the surface of your eyes like the windshield wipers on a car. And like windshield wiper fluid, tears bathe and add moisture to the front of your eyeballs.

Tears contain water, salts, and chemicals that kill germs. The tears are released by **glands** located just above your eyeballs. Most of the time, the liquid either dries or drains into tiny tubes along the inner corner of each eye. If you look at a very bright light or if a speck of dirt blows into your eye, your tear glands give off extra liquid. Some of the tears may spill over your bottom eyelids and run down your cheeks.

◀ *This baby's tears, while showing how unhappy he is, also help keep his eyes moist and clean.*

Inside Your Eyes

Your eyebrows, eyelashes, eyelids, and tears keep the outer layers of your eyes in working order. The **sclera**, or white part of your eye, is also protected by the cornea. The **cornea** is a clear, thin layer that lies on top of the sclera. A layer called the **choroid** lies just below the sclera. It has many tiny blood vessels that bring materials to and remove wastes from the eye cells.

This illustration shows the structures at the front of a person's eyeball. ▶

iris

sclera

pupil

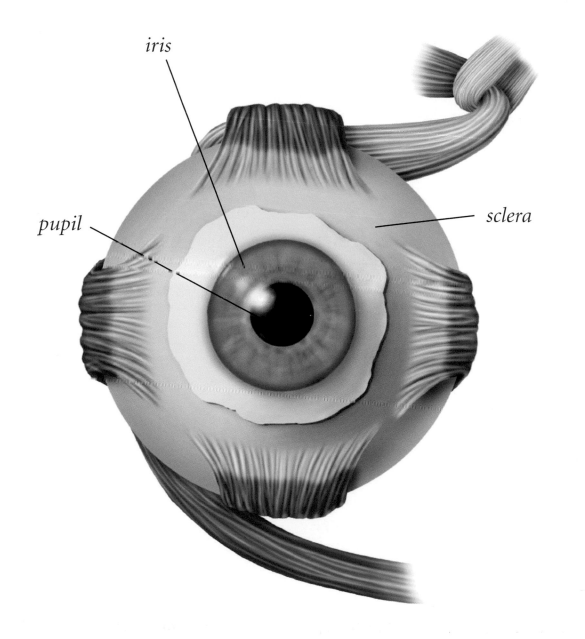

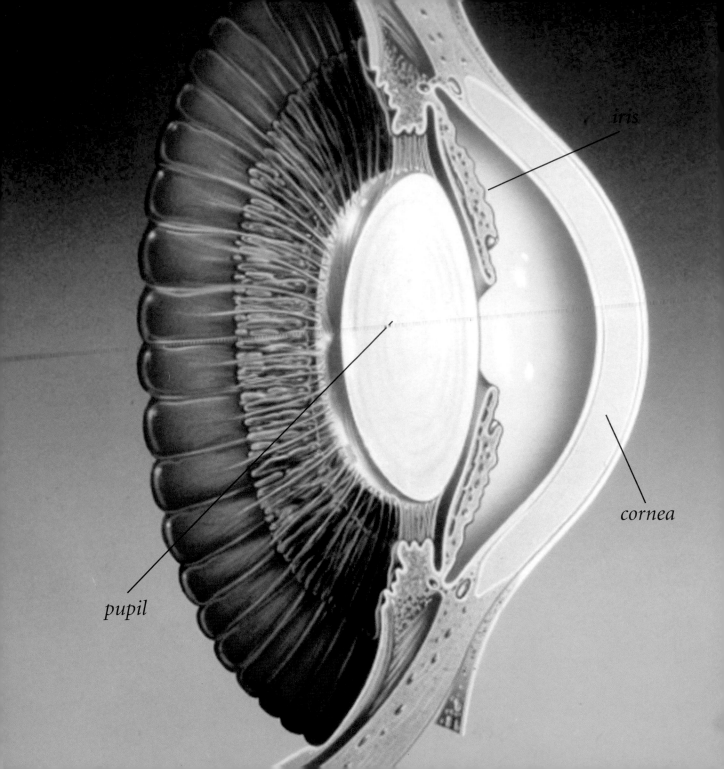

iris

cornea

pupil

At the front of the eye, the choroid merges with the **ciliary body**. The **iris** is a ring-shaped flap of tissue that hangs from the ciliary body. It contains muscles that control the amount of light that enters the inner eye.

As light passes through the cornea, the iris muscles change the size of the **pupil**—a circular opening at the center of the iris. Even though the pupil is like the hole in a doughnut, it looks black because the inside of your eye is dark.

◀ *The pupil lies at the center of the iris. They are both protected by the dome-shaped cornea.*

When you look at a person's eyes, you see the white sclera and the dark central pupil. But what really catches your attention is the colorful iris. Irises can be blue, brown, green, hazel, or even violet. The color depends on the amount of **melanin** in a person's choroid layer. The entire choroid layer is colored, but we can't see most of that color because it is covered by the white sclera.

Behind the iris is a clear, rubbery, pea-sized ball called the **lens**. It is held in place by tough bands of tissue connected to the ciliary body. The ciliary body contains muscles that control the shape of the lens. As the lens changes shape, **images**, or pictures, come into **focus** on a thin layer of tissue that lines the back of the eye. This layer is called the **retina**. The space between the lens and the retina is filled with a clear, jellylike material that helps the eye keep its shape.

This close-up photo shows a person's pupil and iris. ▶

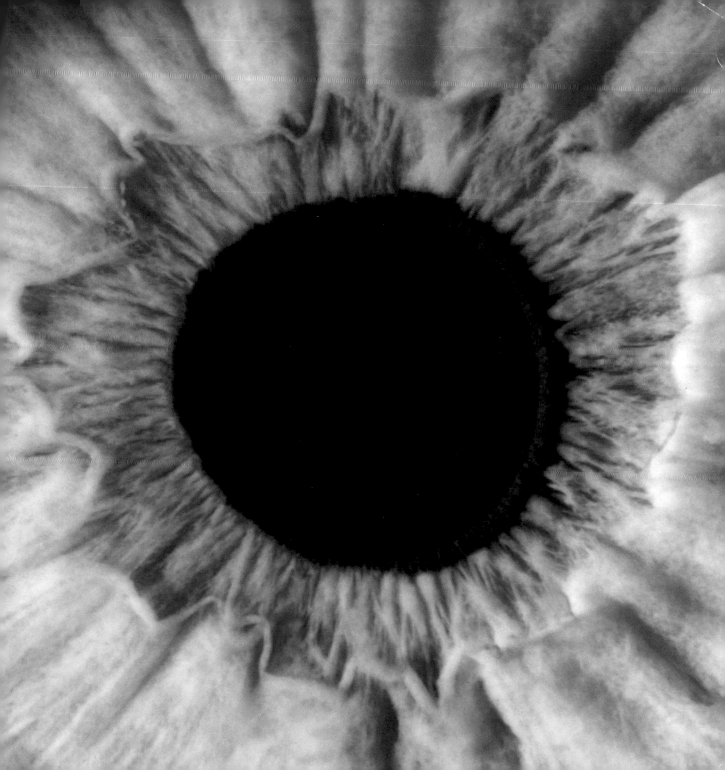

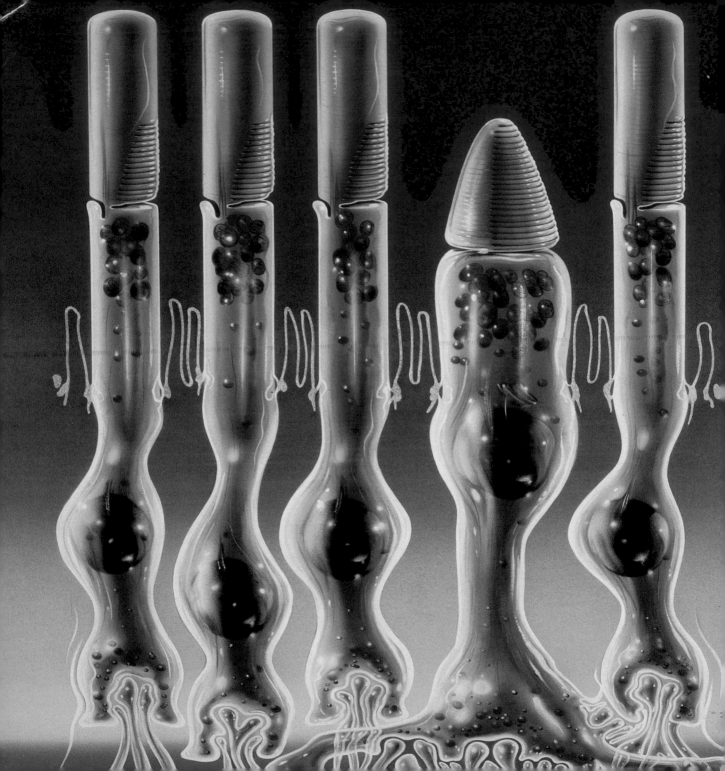

Most of the retina is covered with tightly packed, light-sensitive cells called **rods** and **cones**. Inside each eye, 125 million straight, thin rod cells work in groups to sense tiny pulses of light. Rods help you see shapes and detect movement at night. During the day, your 6 million shorter, plumper cone cells let you see the world in full color. Each cone cell can detect only red, blue, or green light. But when the information gathered by many different cone cells combines in the brain, you can identify more than two hundred different colors.

The surface of your retina is covered with rod and cones. These structures are named for their shape. Rods are long and thin. The tip of a cone looks like an upside-down ice cream cone.

Behind the pupil is the **fovea**—a small dent in the retina that is packed with cone cells. This is the part of the eye that sees objects most clearly in bright daylight. But at night, the fovea is useless. For the best view of an object in dim light, you should look slightly to the side of the object rather than directly at it.

The **optic nerve**—a thick cord of nerves that carries messages from the retina to the brain—enters the eyeball below the fovea. This area of the eye is called the **blind spot** because it has no rod or cone cells to detect light or color.

This photograph was taken with a high-power microscope. It shows the fovea on a person's retina.   ▶

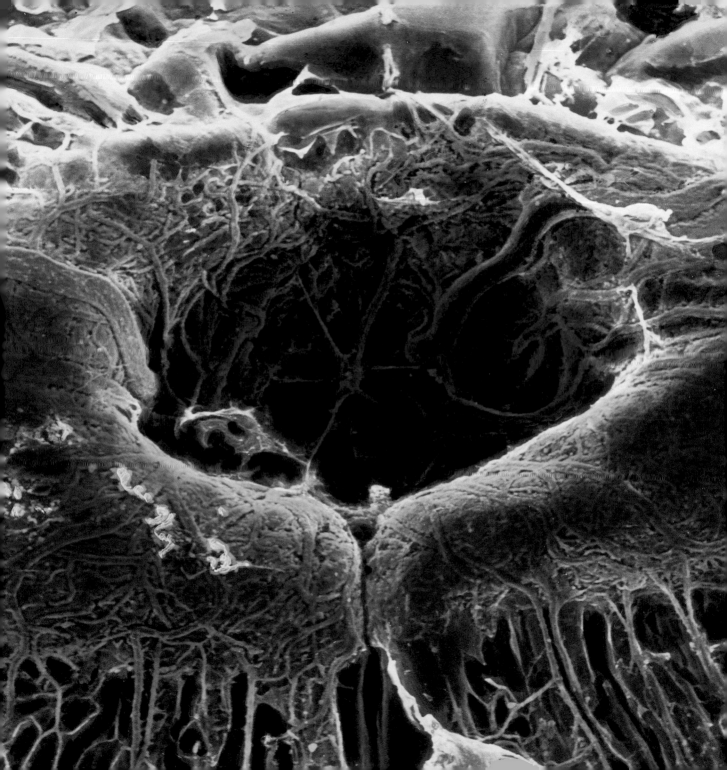

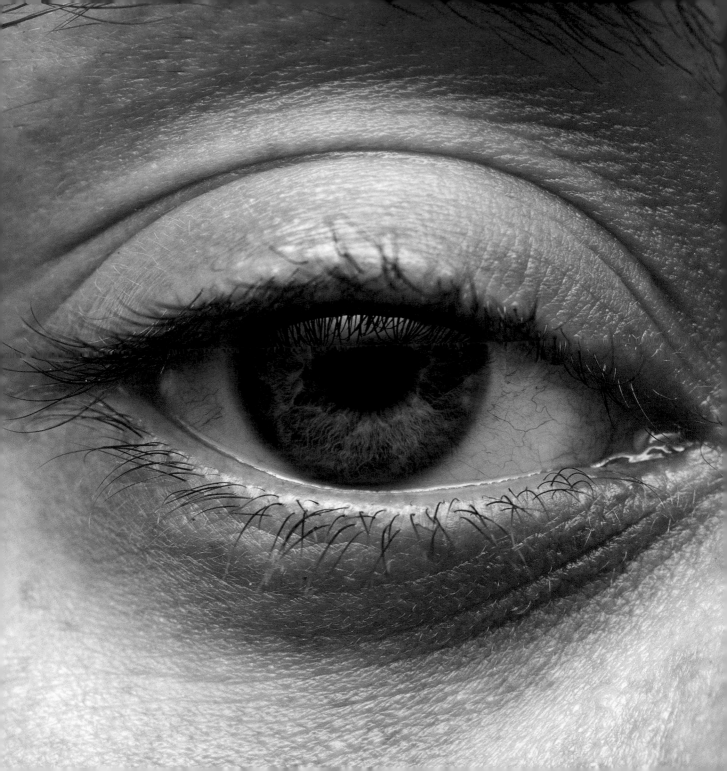

How Your Eyes Work

Sight begins the moment light **reflects** from an object and passes through your cornea. But it is not complete until information about the object is interpreted by your brain. Most of the time, the process takes about one-tenth of a second.

When you are playing outside on a bright, sunny day, there is plenty to see. But too much light can hurt your eyes. By making your pupils smaller, your irises make sure just the right amount of light enters your eyes. But as the sun sets and the sky gets darker, your pupils get larger so more light can pass through them.

To see how this works, look into a mirror, cover your eyes, and count to ten. When you uncover your eyes, watch your pupils closely. You should see them get smaller.

◀ *This photo was taken in medium light, so the person's pupil is average sized.*

Light isn't the only thing that can make pupils get larger or smaller. Your pupils also dilate, or get larger, when you concentrate or feel afraid or excited. Even falling in love can affect the size of a person's pupils.

Whenever light passes through your pupil, it strikes your lens. The lens focuses the light rays by bending them so they meet at a single point and form a clear image on your retina. To focus on a nearby object, such as this book, the muscles in your ciliary body contract. Then your lens becomes rounder and thicker. To see a faraway object, such as an airplane in the sky, the muscles in your ciliary body relax and your lens becomes flatter and thinner.

This person's pupil is extremely large, most likely because there is little light in the room.

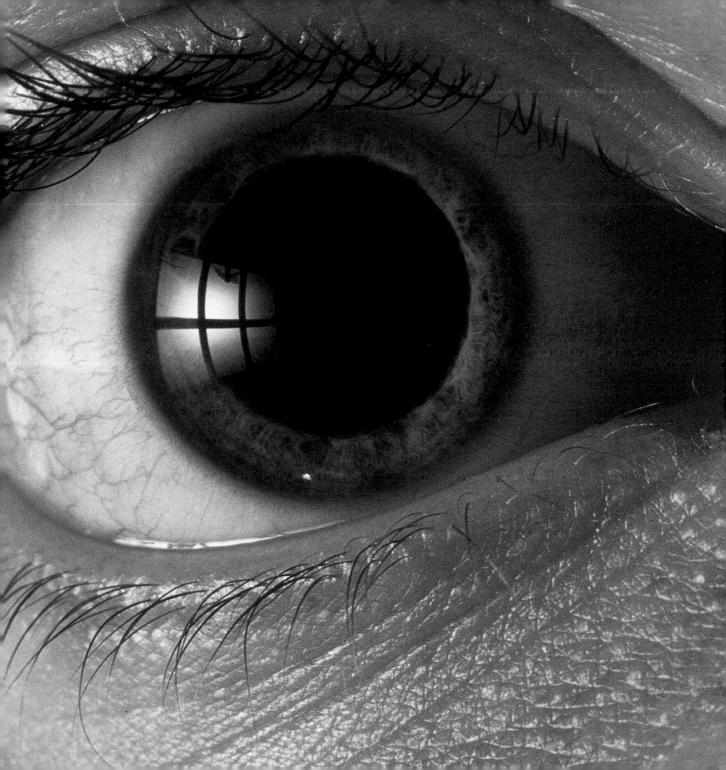

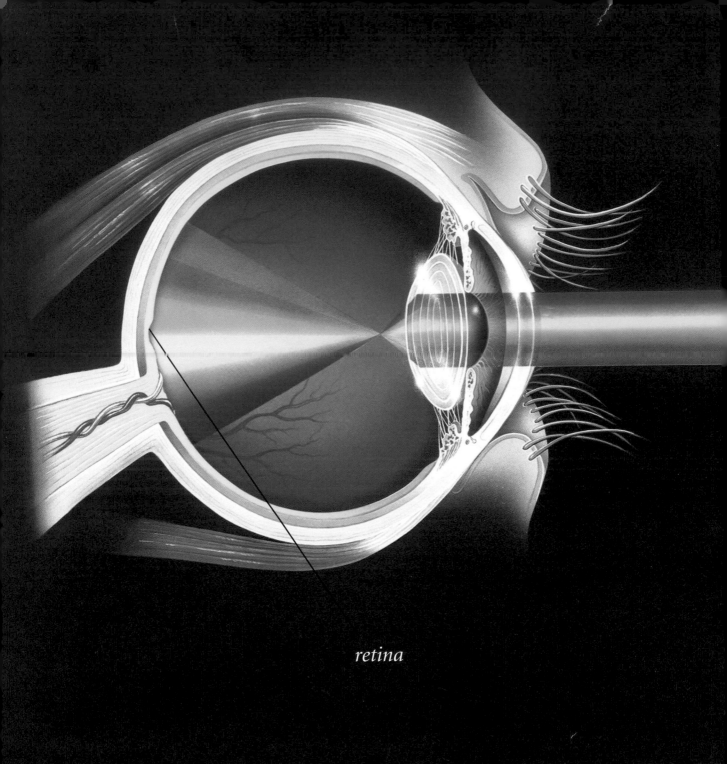

retina

You can feel the muscles in your ciliary body at work. Hold a finger about 6 inches (15 centimeters) in front of your face. Look at the finger for a few seconds, then quickly look out the window. Try this a few times. As your eyes refocus, you should be able to feel a little tug in your eyes. This is your ciliary body working to change the shape of your lenses.

When the lens forms an image on the retina, it is upside down and backward. This image is changed into nerve signals that move along the optic nerve to the **visual cortex** at the back of your brain. If you place your hand on the back of your head, you will be touching the part of your skull that covers and protects the visual cortex.

◀ *When light rays pass through your eye, the lens bends them so they meet at a single point. Then they can form an image on your retina.*

As your visual cortex sorts out and interprets the messages from your eyes, it flips the image so that you see it correctly. The visual cortex also combines nerve messages from both eyes. Even though your eyes are close to one another, each one sees objects from a slightly different angle. By comparing the two images, your brain is able to judge the size and distance of objects. To understand why **three-dimensional vision** is useful, try playing catch with one eye closed. It's not so easy, is it?

Before you can see an object, your brain must receive and interpret messages from your eyes.   ▶

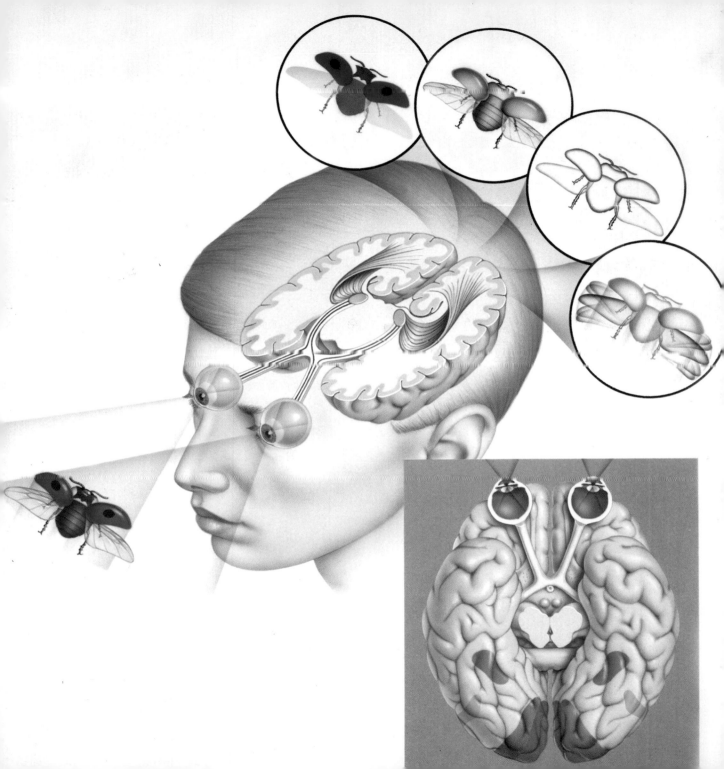

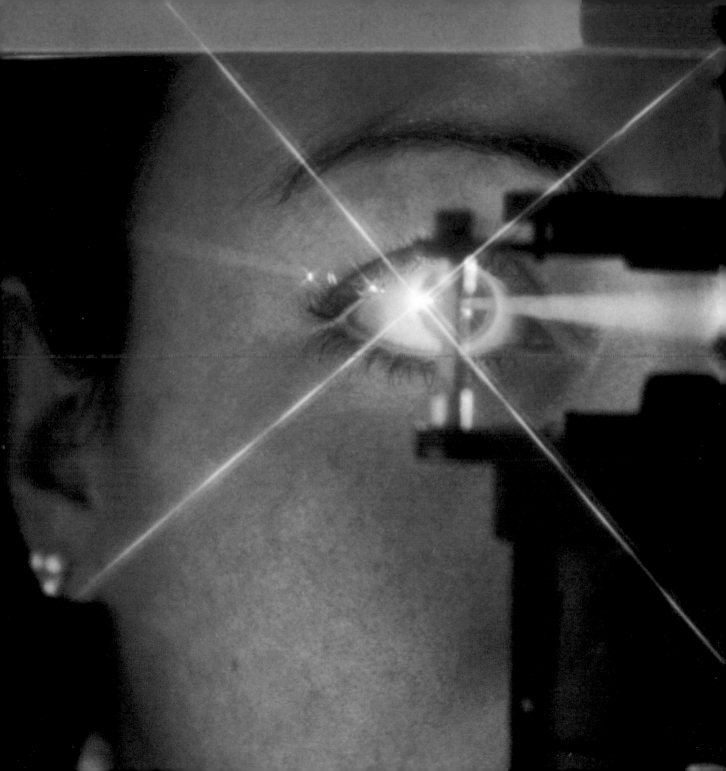

When Eyes Need Help

Even though most people depend on their eyes to understand their surroundings, not everyone has perfect vision. The eye has many parts. If any one of them is the wrong size or shape or cannot do its job, your eyes will not provide a sharp, clear picture of the world.

If a person's cornea is not shaped quite right, light rays will not meet at a single point and form a clear image on the retina. As a result, objects will look blurry. This condition, called **astigmatism**, can be corrected with glasses or contact lenses. Sometimes, it can even be cured by laser surgery, which carefully reshapes the cornea.

◄ *Laser surgery is one way to correct eye problems, such as astigmatism.*

Although the cornea bends light rays a little bit as they enter the eye, the lens does most of the bending. In some people, the lens bends light rays too much or too little for them to focus on the retina. As a result, some objects look blurry. This problem usually happens because a person's eyeball is a little longer or shorter than normal.

If a person's eyeball is too long, focusing on nearby objects is no problem, but distant objects look blurry. This condition is called **myopia**, or nearsightedness. The lens is rubbery and flexible, but it has its limits. In people with myopia, the lens cannot flatten and thin out enough to form an image on the retina. As a result, reflected light rays from distant objects form images before they reach the retina.

If a person's eyeball is a little bit too long or short, objects will look blurry. ▶

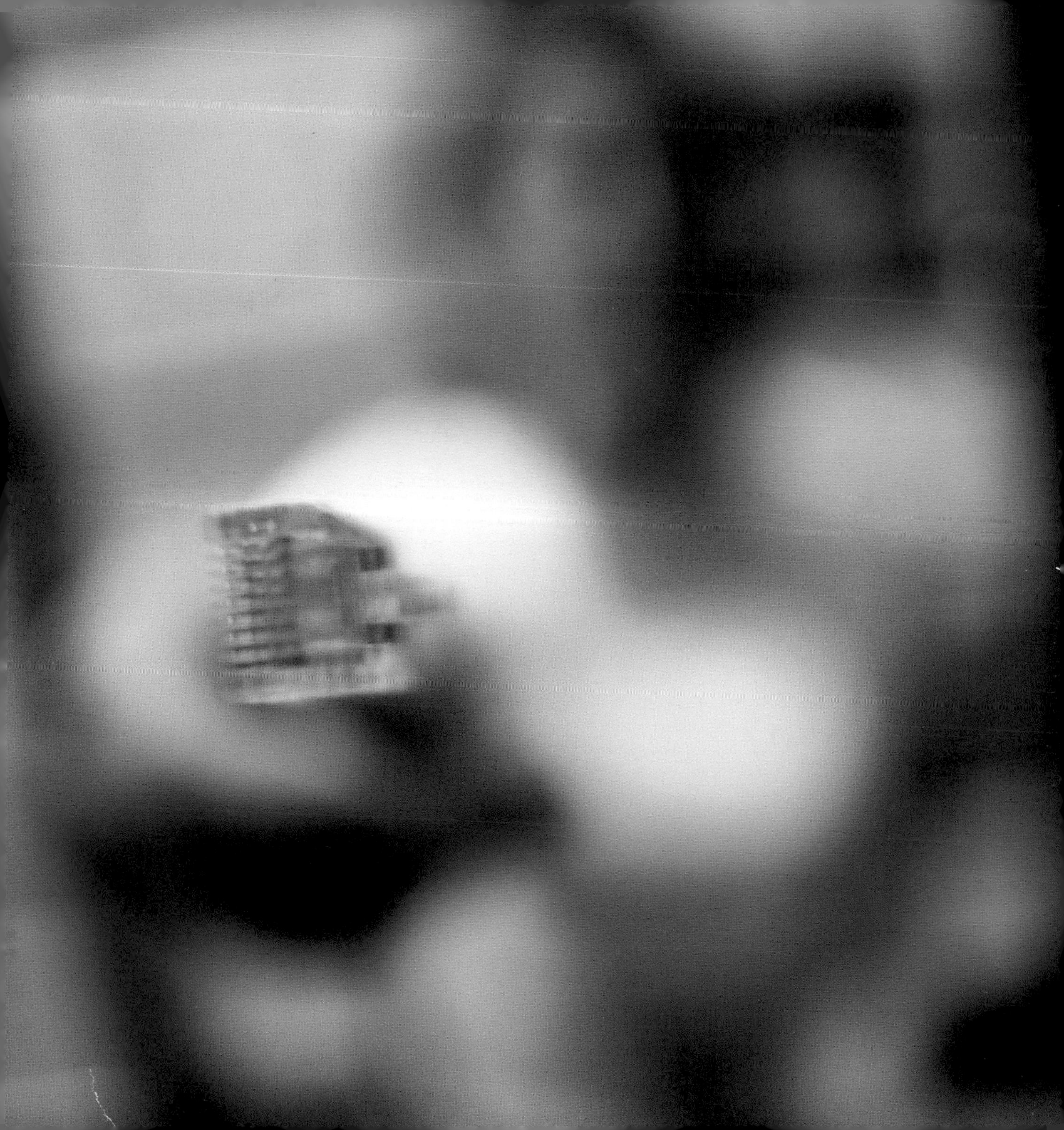

If a person's eyeball is too short, he or she has the opposite problem. Distant objects look clear, but nearby objects are blurry. This condition is called **hyperopia**, or farsightedness. In people with hyperopia, the lens cannot thicken enough to form images of nearby objects on the retina. Instead, the image forms somewhere behind the eyeball.

Both myopia and hyperopia can be corrected by eyeglasses or contact lenses. Nearsighted people wear glasses or contacts lenses that are thin in the center and thick on the edges. When light rays pass through these lenses, they bend outward just enough to form an image on the retina. In farsighted people, the lenses are thick in the middle and thin along the edges. Light rays bend inward just enough to make close objects look crystal clear.

◀ *Eyeglasses help the eye do what it otherwise could not—form clear, sharp images.*

Sometimes objects don't look quite right because there is a problem with the muscles surrounding the eye. If the muscles controlling each eye do not work together, each eye may see slightly different things. When the visual cortex tries to combine the two images, the result is double vision.

Trying to look at two different images at the same time is very confusing. Eventually, the brain will stop gathering information from one eye. When this happens, objects look clear but flat. It is hard to judge exactly how far away they are. This condition is called amblyopia, or lazy eye.

When a person's eye muscles are not working properly, he or she may experience double vision. ▶

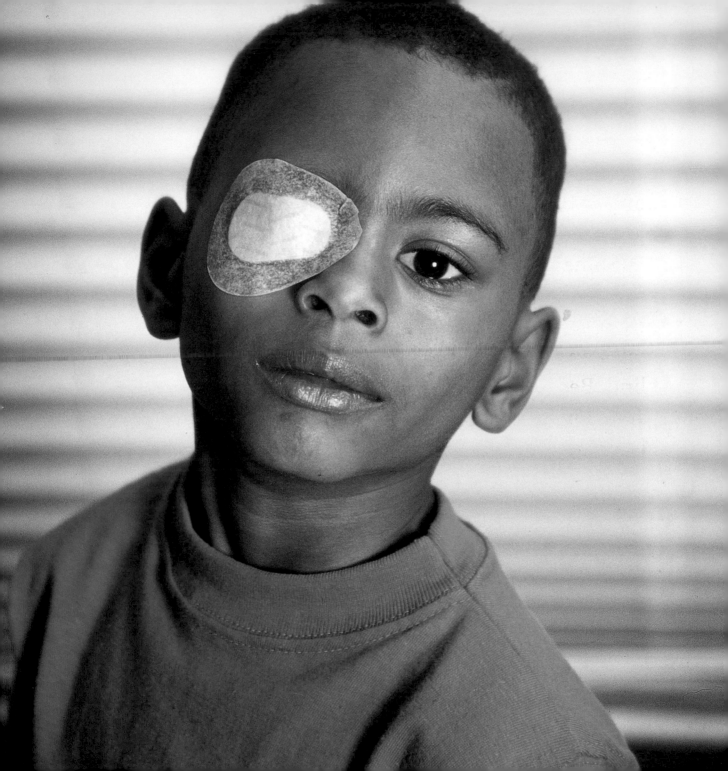

Most people with amblyopia are born that way. If an eye specialist catches the condition early enough, it can be corrected with glasses or by placing an eye patch over the good eye. Once the "lazy" eye learns to see properly, the patch can be removed.

Some people are born with a condition that affects their ability to see colors. **Color blindness** occurs when a person's retina is missing some of its cone cells. Eight percent of all males and one percent of all females are red-green color blind. Because these people have no red or green cones, the two colors look the same to them. There is no cure for color blindness, but people can learn to live with the condition.

◄ *This child wears an eye patch until his "lazy" eye learns to work.*

Keeping Eyes Healthy

Many conditions can affect your eyes for a short time. One of the most common eye diseases is **conjunctivitis**, or pink eye. When the inner lining of the eyelid or the outermost layer of the eyeball is infected, the eye may get red, itchy, and swollen. Sometimes pink eye is the result of an allergy, but it can also be brought on by the same germs that cause colds or sore throats.

Most of the time, pink eye lasts only a few days, but it spreads easily from person to person. If you get pink eye, try not to touch your eyes. Wash your hands often, and do not share towels with other people. If the condition lasts more than a week, you should see a doctor.

It may be hard to avoid pink eye, but there are many simple things you can do to help keep your eyes healthy.

This person is treating conjunctivitis with medicine in a tube. ▶

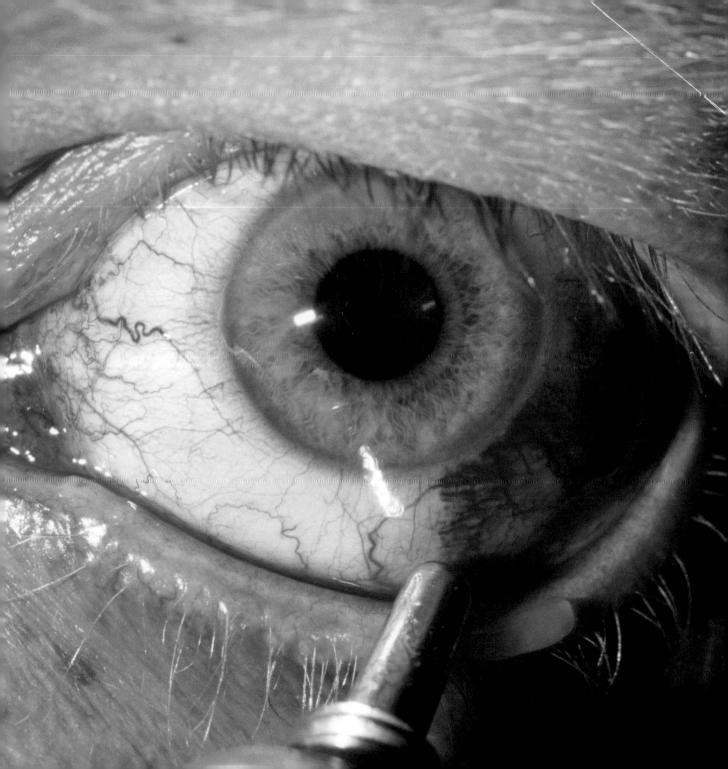

Too much sun can harm your eyes. Never look directly at the sun. If you spend a lot of time outside on sunny days, wear sunglasses and a hat.

To see better at night, drink milk and eat plenty of carrots, cheese, eggs, broccoli, spinach, sweet potatoes, and cantaloupe. These foods are rich in vitamin A. The rod cells on your retinas need vitamin A to work properly.

If you spend too much time staring at a television or computer screen, you may develop eyestrain or dry eye. If things start to look blurry or you get a headache, your eye muscles may be strained. Take a break so your eye muscles can rest.

◀ *Because cantaloupes are rich in vitamin A, they can help keep your eyes healthy.*

Glossary

astigmatism—A condition in which a misshaped cornea makes objects look blurry.

blind spot—The area of the retina that is attached to the optic nerve. It cannot detect light or color because it has no rod or cone cells.

choroid—The layer of the eye that contains many tiny blood vessels, which bring materials to and remove wastes from eye cells.

ciliary body—A part of the eye that has muscles that control the shape of the lens.

color blindness—A condition in which people cannot see certain colors because they were born without some of their cone cells.

cone—A light-sensitive nerve cell on the retina of the eye. In bright light, it allows us to see color.

conjunctivitis—An infection that affects the inside of the eyelid or the topmost layer of the eye.

cornea—The thin, clear layer of tissue that covers the sclera.

focus—To bring into clear view. In the eye, the lens bends light rays to focus images on the retina.

fovea—The area of the retina that sees objects most clearly.

gland—A tiny body part that produces and releases fluids.

hyperopia—Farsightedness; a condition in which distant objects appear clear, but nearby objects look blurry.

image—The way an object appears on the retina.

iris—A ring-shaped flap of muscular tissue that controls the amount of light entering the eye. It also gives the eye its color.

lens—A clear layer of tissue that changes shape to focus images on the retina.

melanin—A molecule that darkens the iris. Brown eyes contain more melanin than blue eyes.

myopia—Nearsightedness; a condition in which close objects appear clear, but distant objects look blurry.

optic nerve—A large nerve that carries messages from the retina to the brain.

pupil—The circular opening in the center of the iris.

reflect—To bounce off.

retina—A thin layer of tissue that lines the back of the eye.

rod—A light-sensitive nerve cell on the retina of the eye. It detects shapes and movement in low light.

three-dimensional vision—In people, combining information from the two eyes so that it is possible to determine the precise location of objects.

sclera—The white outermost layer of the eye.

visual cortex—The area of the brain that processes and interprets messages from the eyes.

Find Out More

Books

Ballard, Carol. *How Do Our Eyes See?* Austin, TX: Raintree/Steck Vaughn, 1998.

Cobb, Vicki. *Open Your Eyes: Discover Your Sense of Sight.* Brookfield, CT: Millbrook Press, 2002.

Gibson, Gary. *Light and Color.* Brookfield, CT: Copper Beech Books, 1995.

Goode, Katherine. *Eyes.* Woodbridge, CT: Blackbirch Press, 2000.

Pringle, Laurence. *Sight.* New York: Benchmark Books, 1999.

Silverstein, Alvin, Virginia Silverstein, and Laura Silverstein Nunn. *Can You See the Chalkboard?* Danbury, CT: Franklin Watts, 2001.

Organizations and Online Sites

National Children's Eye Care Foundation
P.O. Box 795069
Dallas, TX 75379

National Eye Research Foundation
http://www.nerf.org
910 Skokie Blvd., Ste. 207A
Northbrook, IL 60062

National Eye Institute
http://www.nei.nih.gov/
2020 Vision Place
Bethesda, MD 20892

Author's Bio

Beth Ferguson earned a bachelor's degree in biology from Union College and a master's degree in science and environmental journalism from New York University. After working as an editor for many years, she now writes about science and medicine. Ms. Ferguson lives in Massachusetts.

Index